Holy Spirit

WHAT ARE YOU SAYING TO ME?

DAILY JOURNAL

Holy Spirit

WHAT ARE YOU SAYING TO ME?

DAILY JOURNAL

JUAN MARTINEZ

WE ARE
HEAVICANS
PUBLISHING

Published by We are Heavicans
23221 Aldine Westfield Rd
Spring, TX 77373

www.juanmartinez.tv

Identifiers:
ISBN: 979-8-9937654-0-2 (paperback)
ISBN: 979-8-9937654-1-9 (hardback)

Available in paperback and hardback

Unless otherwise stated, all scriptures are taken from the English Standard Version (ESV).

Any Internet addresses (websites, blogs, etc.) and telephone numbers printed in this book are offered as a resource. They are not intended in any way to be or imply an endorsement by the author, nor does the author vouch for the content of these sites and numbers for the life of this book.

Contents

A Note to the Reader

"My sheep hear my voice, and
I know them, and they follow me.

— John 10:27

This journal is an invitation to pause and make space for the voice of the Holy Spirit. The phrase, "Holy Spirit, what are You saying to me?", is a daily reminder to listen, reflect, and allow God to speak personally to your heart. In a world full of noise, it takes intention to slow down and hear His whisper. But when you do, you'll find His words bring peace, direction, and renewal. His power is already at work within you, shaping your thoughts, healing your heart, and guiding your steps. Take your time with these pages. Be real, be open, and let His presence meet you where you are. He's speaking; you just have to lean in and listen.

— Pastor Juan Martinez

Journal

Holy Spirit, What Are You Saying To Me?

Holy Spirit, What Are You Saying To Me?

_____
_____
_____
_____
_____
_____
_____
_____
_____
_____
_____
_____
_____
_____
_____
_____
_____
_____
_____
_____
_____

Holy Spirit, What Are You Saying To Me?

_____
_____
_____
_____
_____
_____
_____
_____
_____
_____
_____
_____
_____
_____
_____
_____
_____
_____
_____
_____
_____
_____
_____
_____
_____
_____
_____

Holy Spirit, What Are You Saying To Me?

_____

_____

_____

_____

_____

_____

_____

_____

_____

_____

_____

_____

_____

_____

_____

_____

_____

_____

_____

_____

_____

_____

_____

Holy Spirit, What Are You Saying To Me?

Holy Spirit, What Are You Saying To Me?

Holy Spirit, What Are You Saying To Me?

Holy Spirit, What Are You Saying To Me?

_____

_____

_____

_____

_____

_____

_____

_____

_____

_____

_____

_____

_____

_____

_____

_____

_____

_____

_____

_____

_____

_____

Holy Spirit, What Are You Saying To Me?

Holy Spirit, What Are You Saying To Me?

Holy Spirit, What Are You Saying To Me?

Holy Spirit, What Are You Saying To Me?

Holy Spirit, What Are You Saying To Me?

Holy Spirit, What Are You Saying To Me?

_____
_____
_____
_____
_____
_____
_____
_____
_____
_____
_____
_____
_____
_____
_____
_____
_____
_____
_____

Holy Spirit, What Are You Saying To Me?

Holy Spirit, What Are You Saying To Me?

_____

_____

_____

_____

_____

_____

_____

_____

_____

_____

_____

_____

_____

_____

_____

_____

_____

_____

_____

_____

_____

_____

_____

_____

Holy Spirit, What Are You Saying To Me?

Holy Spirit, What Are You Saying To Me?

Holy Spirit, What Are You Saying To Me?

Holy Spirit, What Are You Saying To Me?

Holy Spirit, What Are You Saying To Me?

Holy Spirit, What Are You Saying To Me?

Holy Spirit, What Are You Saying To Me?

Holy Spirit, What Are You Saying To Me?

Holy Spirit, What Are You Saying To Me?

_____
_____
_____
_____
_____
_____
_____
_____
_____
_____
_____
_____
_____
_____
_____
_____
_____
_____
_____
_____
_____
_____
_____
_____

Holy Spirit, What Are You Saying To Me?

Holy Spirit, What Are You Saying To Me?

Holy Spirit, What Are You Saying To Me?

Holy Spirit, What Are You Saying To Me?

Holy Spirit, What Are You Saying To Me?

Holy Spirit, What Are You Saying To Me?

Holy Spirit, What Are You Saying To Me?

Holy Spirit, What Are You Saying To Me?

_____

_____

_____

_____

_____

_____

_____

_____

_____

_____

_____

_____

_____

_____

_____

_____

_____

_____

_____

_____

_____

_____

_____

_____

_____

_____

Holy Spirit, What Are You Saying To Me?

Holy Spirit, What Are You Saying To Me?

Holy Spirit, What Are You Saying To Me?

Holy Spirit, What Are You Saying To Me?

Holy Spirit, What Are You Saying To Me?

Holy Spirit, What Are You Saying To Me?

Holy Spirit, What Are You Saying To Me?

_____
_____
_____
_____
_____
_____
_____
_____
_____
_____
_____
_____
_____
_____
_____
_____
_____
_____
_____
_____
_____
_____
_____
_____
_____
_____
_____

Holy Spirit, What Are You Saying To Me?

Holy Spirit, What Are You Saying To Me?

_____

_____

_____

_____

_____

_____

_____

_____

_____

_____

_____

_____

_____

_____

_____

_____

_____

_____

_____

_____

_____

_____

Holy Spirit, What Are You Saying To Me?

Holy Spirit, What Are You Saying To Me?

Holy Spirit, What Are You Saying To Me?

Holy Spirit, What Are You Saying To Me?

Holy Spirit, What Are You Saying To Me?

Holy Spirit, What Are You Saying To Me?

_____
_____
_____
_____
_____
_____
_____
_____
_____
_____
_____
_____
_____
_____
_____
_____
_____
_____
_____
_____
_____
_____
_____
_____
_____
_____

Holy Spirit, What Are You Saying To Me?

Holy Spirit, What Are You Saying To Me?

_____
_____
_____
_____
_____
_____
_____
_____
_____
_____
_____
_____
_____
_____
_____
_____
_____
_____
_____
_____
_____
_____

Holy Spirit, What Are You Saying To Me?

_____
_____
_____
_____
_____
_____
_____
_____
_____
_____
_____
_____
_____
_____
_____
_____
_____
_____
_____
_____
_____
_____
_____
_____
_____
_____
_____
_____
_____

Holy Spirit, What Are You Saying To Me?

Holy Spirit, What Are You Saying To Me?

Holy Spirit, What Are You Saying To Me?

_____

_____

_____

_____

_____

_____

_____

_____

_____

_____

_____

_____

_____

_____

_____

_____

_____

_____

_____

_____

_____

_____

_____

Holy Spirit, What Are You Saying To Me?

Holy Spirit, What Are You Saying To Me?

Holy Spirit, What Are You Saying To Me?

Holy Spirit, What Are You Saying To Me?

Holy Spirit, What Are You Saying To Me?

_____
_____
_____
_____
_____
_____
_____
_____
_____
_____
_____
_____
_____
_____
_____
_____
_____
_____
_____
_____
_____
_____
_____
_____
_____

Holy Spirit, What Are You Saying To Me?

_____

_____

_____

_____

_____

_____

_____

_____

_____

_____

_____

_____

_____

_____

_____

_____

_____

_____

_____

_____

_____

_____

_____

_____

Holy Spirit, What Are You Saying To Me?

_____

_____

_____

_____

_____

_____

_____

_____

_____

_____

_____

_____

_____

_____

_____

_____

_____

_____

_____

_____

_____

_____

_____

_____

_____

_____

_____

Holy Spirit, What Are You Saying To Me?

Holy Spirit, What Are You Saying To Me?

Holy Spirit, What Are You Saying To Me?

Holy Spirit, What Are You Saying To Me?

Holy Spirit, What Are You Saying To Me?

Holy Spirit, What Are You Saying To Me?

Holy Spirit, What Are You Saying To Me?

Holy Spirit, What Are You Saying To Me?

Holy Spirit, What Are You Saying To Me?

Holy Spirit, What Are You Saying To Me?

Holy Spirit, What Are You Saying To Me?

_____

_____

_____

_____

_____

_____

_____

_____

_____

_____

_____

_____

_____

_____

_____

_____

_____

_____

_____

_____

_____

_____

_____

_____

Holy Spirit, What Are You Saying To Me?

_____

_____

_____

_____

_____

_____

_____

_____

_____

_____

_____

_____

_____

_____

_____

_____

_____

_____

_____

_____

_____

_____

_____

_____

_____

_____

_____

Holy Spirit, What Are You Saying To Me?

_____

_____

_____

_____

_____

_____

_____

_____

_____

_____

_____

_____

_____

_____

_____

_____

_____

_____

_____

_____

_____

_____

Holy Spirit, What Are You Saying To Me?

Holy Spirit, What Are You Saying To Me?

_____

_____

_____

_____

_____

_____

_____

_____

_____

_____

_____

_____

_____

_____

_____

_____

_____

_____

_____

_____

_____

_____

Holy Spirit, What Are You Saying To Me?

Holy Spirit, What Are You Saying To Me?

Holy Spirit, What Are You Saying To Me?

Holy Spirit, What Are You Saying To Me?

Holy Spirit, What Are You Saying To Me?

Holy Spirit, What Are You Saying To Me?

_____

_____

_____

_____

_____

_____

_____

_____

_____

_____

_____

_____

_____

_____

_____

_____

_____

_____

_____

_____

_____

Holy Spirit, What Are You Saying To Me?

Holy Spirit, What Are You Saying To Me?

Holy Spirit, What Are You Saying To Me?

_____

_____

_____

_____

_____

_____

_____

_____

_____

_____

_____

_____

_____

_____

_____

_____

_____

_____

_____

_____

_____

_____

_____

Holy Spirit, What Are You Saying To Me?

Holy Spirit, What Are You Saying To Me?

Holy Spirit, What Are You Saying To Me?

Holy Spirit, What Are You Saying To Me?

Holy Spirit, What Are You Saying To Me?

Holy Spirit, What Are You Saying To Me?

_____

_____

_____

_____

_____

_____

_____

_____

_____

_____

_____

_____

_____

_____

_____

_____

_____

_____

_____

_____

_____

_____

_____

_____

_____

Holy Spirit, What Are You Saying To Me?

_____

_____

_____

_____

_____

_____

_____

_____

_____

_____

_____

_____

_____

_____

_____

_____

_____

_____

_____

_____

_____

_____

_____

Holy Spirit, What Are You Saying To Me?

Holy Spirit, What Are You Saying To Me?

_____

_____

_____

_____

_____

_____

_____

_____

_____

_____

_____

_____

_____

_____

_____

_____

_____

_____

_____

_____

_____

_____

_____

_____

Holy Spirit, What Are You Saying To Me?

Holy Spirit, What Are You Saying To Me?

_____
_____
_____
_____
_____
_____
_____
_____
_____
_____
_____
_____
_____
_____
_____
_____
_____
_____
_____
_____
_____

Holy Spirit, What Are You Saying To Me?

Holy Spirit, What Are You Saying To Me?

_____

_____

_____

_____

_____

_____

_____

_____

_____

_____

_____

_____

_____

_____

_____

_____

_____

_____

_____

_____

_____

_____

_____

_____

Holy Spirit, What Are You Saying To Me?

Holy Spirit, What Are You Saying To Me?

Holy Spirit, What Are You Saying To Me?

Holy Spirit, What Are You Saying To Me?

Holy Spirit, What Are You Saying To Me?

_____
_____
_____
_____
_____
_____
_____
_____
_____
_____
_____
_____
_____
_____
_____
_____
_____
_____
_____
_____
_____
_____

Holy Spirit, What Are You Saying To Me?

Holy Spirit, What Are You Saying To Me?

Holy Spirit, What Are You Saying To Me?

Holy Spirit, What Are You Saying To Me?

Holy Spirit, What Are You Saying To Me?

_____
_____
_____
_____
_____
_____
_____
_____
_____
_____
_____
_____
_____
_____
_____
_____
_____
_____
_____
_____
_____
_____
_____
_____

Holy Spirit, What Are You Saying To Me?

Holy Spirit, What Are You Saying To Me?

_____
_____
_____
_____
_____
_____
_____
_____
_____
_____
_____
_____
_____
_____
_____
_____
_____
_____
_____
_____
_____
_____
_____

Holy Spirit, What Are You Saying To Me?

_____

_____

_____

_____

_____

_____

_____

_____

_____

_____

_____

_____

_____

_____

_____

_____

_____

_____

_____

_____

_____

_____

Holy Spirit, What Are You Saying To Me?

_____
_____
_____
_____
_____
_____
_____
_____
_____
_____
_____
_____
_____
_____
_____
_____
_____
_____
_____
_____
_____
_____
_____

Holy Spirit, What Are You Saying To Me?

Holy Spirit, What Are You Saying To Me?

Holy Spirit, What Are You Saying To Me?

_____

_____

_____

_____

_____

_____

_____

_____

_____

_____

_____

_____

_____

_____

_____

_____

_____

_____

_____

_____

_____

_____

Holy Spirit, What Are You Saying To Me?

Holy Spirit, What Are You Saying To Me?

_____

_____

_____

_____

_____

_____

_____

_____

_____

_____

_____

_____

_____

_____

_____

_____

_____

_____

_____

_____

_____

_____

Holy Spirit, What Are You Saying To Me?

Holy Spirit, What Are You Saying To Me?

Holy Spirit, What Are You Saying To Me?

_____

_____

_____

_____

_____

_____

_____

_____

_____

_____

_____

_____

_____

_____

_____

_____

_____

_____

_____

_____

_____

_____

Holy Spirit, What Are You Saying To Me?

Holy Spirit, What Are You Saying To Me?

Holy Spirit, What Are You Saying To Me?

Holy Spirit, What Are You Saying To Me?

Holy Spirit, What Are You Saying To Me?

_____

_____

_____

_____

_____

_____

_____

_____

_____

_____

_____

_____

_____

_____

_____

_____

_____

_____

_____

_____

_____

_____

_____

_____

_____

_____

_____

Holy Spirit, What Are You Saying To Me?

Holy Spirit, What Are You Saying To Me?

_____

_____

_____

_____

_____

_____

_____

_____

_____

_____

_____

_____

_____

_____

_____

_____

_____

_____

_____

_____

_____

_____

_____

_____

_____

_____

_____

_____

Holy Spirit, What Are You Saying To Me?

Holy Spirit, What Are You Saying To Me?

Holy Spirit, What Are You Saying To Me?

Holy Spirit, What Are You Saying To Me?

_____

_____

_____

_____

_____

_____

_____

_____

_____

_____

_____

_____

_____

_____

_____

_____

_____

_____

_____

_____

_____

_____

Holy Spirit, What Are You Saying To Me?

Holy Spirit, What Are You Saying To Me?

Holy Spirit, What Are You Saying To Me?

_____

_____

_____

_____

_____

_____

_____

_____

_____

_____

_____

_____

_____

_____

_____

_____

_____

_____

_____

_____

_____

_____

_____

_____

Holy Spirit, What Are You Saying To Me?

Holy Spirit, What Are You Saying To Me?

_____

_____

_____

_____

_____

_____

_____

_____

_____

_____

_____

_____

_____

_____

_____

_____

_____

_____

_____

_____

_____

_____

_____

Holy Spirit, What Are You Saying To Me?

Holy Spirit, What Are You Saying To Me?

_____
_____
_____
_____
_____
_____
_____
_____
_____
_____
_____
_____
_____
_____
_____
_____
_____
_____
_____
_____
_____
_____

Holy Spirit, What Are You Saying To Me?

Holy Spirit, What Are You Saying To Me?

_____

_____

_____

_____

_____

_____

_____

_____

_____

_____

_____

_____

_____

_____

_____

_____

_____

_____

_____

_____

_____

Holy Spirit, What Are You Saying To Me?

Holy Spirit, What Are You Saying To Me?

_____

_____

_____

_____

_____

_____

_____

_____

_____

_____

_____

_____

_____

_____

_____

_____

_____

_____

_____

_____

_____

Holy Spirit, What Are You Saying To Me?

Holy Spirit, What Are You Saying To Me?

Holy Spirit, What Are You Saying To Me?

Holy Spirit, What Are You Saying To Me?

_____

_____

_____

_____

_____

_____

_____

_____

_____

_____

_____

_____

_____

_____

_____

_____

_____

_____

_____

_____

_____

_____

Holy Spirit, What Are You Saying To Me?

_____

_____

_____

_____

_____

_____

_____

_____

_____

_____

_____

_____

_____

_____

_____

_____

_____

_____

_____

_____

_____

_____

_____

_____

Holy Spirit, What Are You Saying To Me?

Holy Spirit, What Are You Saying To Me?

Holy Spirit, What Are You Saying To Me?

Holy Spirit, What Are You Saying To Me?

_____

_____

_____

_____

_____

_____

_____

_____

_____

_____

_____

_____

_____

_____

_____

_____

_____

_____

_____

_____

_____

_____

_____

_____

_____

_____

Holy Spirit, What Are You Saying To Me?

Holy Spirit, What Are You Saying To Me?

_____
_____
_____
_____
_____
_____
_____
_____
_____
_____
_____
_____
_____
_____
_____
_____
_____
_____
_____
_____
_____
_____
_____
_____

Holy Spirit, What Are You Saying To Me?

_____

_____

_____

_____

_____

_____

_____

_____

_____

_____

_____

_____

_____

_____

_____

_____

_____

_____

_____

_____

_____

_____

Holy Spirit, What Are You Saying To Me?

_____

_____

_____

_____

_____

_____

_____

_____

_____

_____

_____

_____

_____

_____

_____

_____

_____

_____

_____

_____

_____

Holy Spirit, What Are You Saying To Me?

Holy Spirit, What Are You Saying To Me?

Holy Spirit, What Are You Saying To Me?

_____
_____
_____
_____
_____
_____
_____
_____
_____
_____
_____
_____
_____
_____
_____
_____
_____
_____
_____
_____

Holy Spirit, What Are You Saying To Me?

Holy Spirit, What Are You Saying To Me?

Holy Spirit, What Are You Saying To Me?

Holy Spirit, What Are You Saying To Me?

Holy Spirit, What Are You Saying To Me?

_____

_____

_____

_____

_____

_____

_____

_____

_____

_____

_____

_____

_____

_____

_____

_____

_____

_____

_____

_____

_____

_____

_____

_____

_____

Holy Spirit, What Are You Saying To Me?

Holy Spirit, What Are You Saying To Me?

_____
_____
_____
_____
_____
_____
_____
_____
_____
_____
_____
_____
_____
_____
_____
_____
_____
_____
_____
_____
_____
_____
_____

Holy Spirit, What Are You Saying To Me?

Holy Spirit, What Are You Saying To Me?

Holy Spirit, What Are You Saying To Me?

Holy Spirit, What Are You Saying To Me?

_____

_____

_____

_____

_____

_____

_____

_____

_____

_____

_____

_____

_____

_____

_____

_____

_____

_____

_____

_____

_____

_____

_____

_____

_____

Holy Spirit, What Are You Saying To Me?

Holy Spirit, What Are You Saying To Me?

_____

_____

_____

_____

_____

_____

_____

_____

_____

_____

_____

_____

_____

_____

_____

_____

_____

_____

_____

_____

_____

_____

_____

_____

Holy Spirit, What Are You Saying To Me?

_____
_____
_____
_____
_____
_____
_____
_____
_____
_____
_____
_____
_____
_____
_____
_____
_____
_____
_____
_____
_____
_____
_____
_____

Holy Spirit, What Are You Saying To Me?

_____

_____

_____

_____

_____

_____

_____

_____

_____

_____

_____

_____

_____

_____

_____

_____

_____

_____

_____

_____

_____

_____

_____

_____

Holy Spirit, What Are You Saying To Me?

_____

_____

_____

_____

_____

_____

_____

_____

_____

_____

_____

_____

_____

_____

_____

_____

_____

_____

_____

_____

_____

_____

Holy Spirit, What Are You Saying To Me?

Holy Spirit, What Are You Saying To Me?

Holy Spirit, What Are You Saying To Me?

_____

_____

_____

_____

_____

_____

_____

_____

_____

_____

_____

_____

_____

_____

_____

_____

_____

_____

_____

_____

Holy Spirit, What Are You Saying To Me?

Holy Spirit, What Are You Saying To Me?

Holy Spirit, What Are You Saying To Me?

About the Author

Juan Martinez, lead pastor of Get Wrapped Church and founder of *Love Live Lead Ministries*, is a revivalist passionate about reaching the lost and broken. A radio and TV host featured on TBN and CTN, he's a popular conference speaker and author of *Beyond the Yellow Brick Road*, *Prison Break*, and *That's Crazy No, that's God!* Juan lives in Houston with his wife, Ruthy, and their six children.

OTHER BOOKS FROM JUAM MARTINEZ

PRISON BREAK

After experiencing the realities of a physical prison cell, Pastor Juan Martinez has made it his mission to help others find freedom in every way possible—spiritually, culturally, emotionally, psychologically, and physically.

Encouraging life change through practical steps—such as challenging negative thinking patterns with positive affirmations and setting realistic goals—this twenty-one-day devotional helps expose the internal anxiety, faulty thinking, and traumas that put readers behind figurative or literal bars, causing them to repeatedly make bad decisions and experience relationship challenges. Readers will recognize the root causes of the psychological chains breaking them so they can reach greater personal growth. Prison Break serves as a poignant reminder that freedom is possible and shows readers that with the right mindset, they can overcome past mistakes, forgive others, be renewed by the transformation of their minds, and lead a fulfilling life.

THAT'S CRAZY No, That's God!

While reading this book, you will step out of your self-imposed limitations and experience the truly extraordinary workings of God.

From Noah building an ark in a dry land to Peter stepping out of the boat, God's plans have always defied human logic. Through powerful testimonies and biblical teaching, Pastor Juan Martinez challenges believers to stop limiting God with small thinking and instead embrace the extraordinary.

That's Crazy—No, That's God is a powerful invitation for readers to step out of the ordinary and into a life marked by the miraculous. Many have heard the words, "That's crazy!" when sharing a vision or calling from God.

www.ingramcontent.com/pod-product-compliance
Lightning Source LLC
Chambersburg PA
CBHW070916130626
46555CB00001B/161